CHICHÉN- ITZÁ
TULUM AND COBÁ

yesterday
&
TODAY

The most important temple

UNIVERSAL IMAGE ENTERPRISES

GRAPHICS
AND PHOTOGRAPHY
Immagine Universale
e-mail: immagineuniversale@libero.it

CONTENTS

Map of the Maya Area

RIO LAGARTOS

YUCATAN

CANCUN

CELESTUN

CHICHÉN ITZÁ

UXMAL

COBA

KABAH
SAYIL

LABNÁ

TULUM

GULF
OF MEXICO

EDZNÁ

HOCHOB

QUINTANA
ROO

CAMPECHE

BECÁN

CHICANNÁ

XPUJIL

KOHUNLICH

COMALCALCO

CARIBBEAN
SEA

TABASCO

PALENQUE

ALTUN HA

AGUA
AZUL

TIKAL

BELIZE

YAXCHILÁN

SAN CRISTOBAL
DE LAS CASAS

BONAMPAK

CHIAPAS

GUATEMALA

COPÁN

HONDURAS

ANTIGUA

PACIFIC
OCEAN

TAZUMAL

EL SALVADOR

THE CITY OF CHICHÉN ITZÁ

The ancient city of Chichén Itzá stands on the Yucatan peninsula in the state of Yucatan at about 120 km from its capital, Merida. It can be reached from the capital or from Cancun by highway 180 or the toll road, or by air on daily flights by local companies.

Chichén Itzácovers an area of 15 square kilometres and has 15 ball game courts including the largest ever found in Central America.

The city has 5 separate squares, of which only three have been restored. The other two are at Old Chichén, along with the Temple of the Date and the Temple of the Phallus. All the squares are connected by 'sacbe', official roads from 3 to 8 metres wide.

John Lloyd Stephens and Frederick Catherwood left us a marvellous description in words and pictures, of Chichén Itza as they found it in 1842. They were the first of a long line of adventurers, photographers, artists and archaeologists to visit the area in the eighteenth century: Charnay, Augustus and Alice Le Plongeon,

Maudslay, Maler, Holnes and Breton.

At the dawn of the twentieth century, Edward H. Thompson excavated some structures, with great material results but little technique, and dredged the sacred well.

Seler, Tozzer and Marquiña classified the iconography and architecture of the site in order to undertake comparative studies and when the Mexican government (from 1924 onwards) and the Carnegie Institute (from 1923

Sculpture of Chac mool, of Toltec influence, found in Chichén Itzá and kept in the Archaeological Museum in Merida.

The name Chichén Itzá can be divided into three words of the Itza-Maya dialect: "Chi", "Chén" and "Itzá", which respectively mean "Mouth", "Well" and "Itza people". Hence the mouth of the well of the Itzá.

It is probable that the well referred to is the famous sacred well, about which so much has been written.

Map of Chichén Itzá

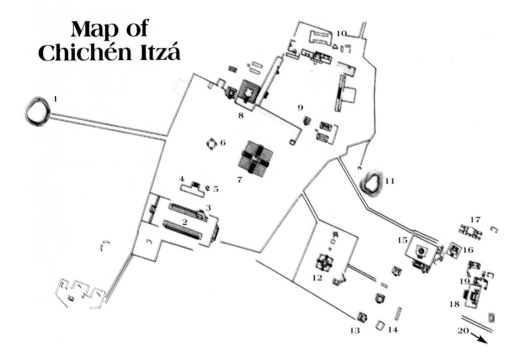

1	Sacred well	11	Xtóloc well
2	Ball game	12	Ossuary
3	Temple of the Jaguars	13	Temple of the Deer
4	Tzompantli	14	Red House
5	Temple of the Eagles	15	Caracol
6	Temple of Venus	16	Halls of matematics and Philosophy
7	Castle	17	Akab-Dzib
8	Temple of the Warriors	18	Temple of the Nuns
9	Group of the Thousand Columns	19	Iglesia
10	Steam Bath	20	Old Chichén

to 1936) sent research groups to the site, the major restorations began.

Chichén Itzá was a major site for the teaching of philosophy, science and the arts.

Every building had a function related to these disciplines and courses of study aimed at training better and more knowledgeable human beings.

The city can be divided into two parts, the first, the religious section, comprises the **Ball Game**, the **Tzomplanti Temple**, the **Temple of the Eagles**, the **Temple of Venus**, the **Pyramid of Kukulcan**, the **Sacred Well** (*Cenote Sagrado*), the **Temple of the Warriors** (with the so-called annexes), the **Ossuary** (with its funerary footpath) and **Old Chichén** (*with the Temple of the Date, the Temple of the Phallus and other structures*).

The second section is the scientific one, which comprises the **House of the Deer** (*Venado*), the **Astronomical Observatory** (*Caracol*), the **Church** (*Iglesias*), the **Monastery** (*Las Monjas*) and the **Akab-Dzib** (*occult writing*).

Chichén Itza, long considered an immense treasure, has been declared unequivocally a Cultural Asset of Humanity.

Plate 1 - Chichén Itzá: aerial view of the ceremonial area

The Ball Game

The Ball Game proper is 146 metres long and 36 m wide, while the entire enclosure, inclusive of the temples north and south, measures 168 m in length by 70 m in breadth.

The ball court is flanked east and west by long platforms from which rise boundary walls to mark out the field.

The walls of both platforms are composed of three panels with a border formed by a bas-relief representing a serpent, which terminates with a head at each end.

In the centre of both walls of the game, at a height of 8 metres, there are two stone rings in the form of intertwined serpents.

The temple on the north side of

Photo above: Game of ball with detail of the Temple of the Jaguars

On the right, ceramic figures from the Island of Jaina, representing two ball players

the ball field, which rests on a platform 14 x 8 metres, is called simply the North Temple or the Temple of the Bearded Man, from one of the two figures carved on its walls.

On the opposite side one finds the South Temple, which rests on a rectangular foundation 25 x 8 metres. One can admire six columns on which there are carved figures that might signify men who had reached the level of great Master Quetzalcoatl, serpent-bird.

The Temple of the Jaguars, situated at the southern extremity of the east flank of the enclosure, was used, among other things, as the principal stand for spectators. Its two columns have the form of gigantic serpents, with the head at the base and the jaws wide open.

Plate 2 - Chichén Itzá: the Temple of the Jaguars

Tzompantli

The Tzompantli is a rectangular platform that measures 60 metres by 12, accessed by a short corridor that starts eastwards from the centre of the structure.

Seen from above it appears as a great capital T, with the horizontal stroke very much longer than the vertical. The walls of the platform are carved with skulls, the entrance-exit with eagles.

Unfortunately the skulls capture the popular imagination and that of not a few researchers, so that many fantastic theories have been put about. One of the most colourful says that the heads of sacrificial victims were exposed here, but the Maya people suggest that they was too developed to indulge in such manifestations.

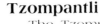

Temple of the Eagles

The Temple of the Eagles is a solid square platform with four stairs, each adorned with two huge serpent heads. Wide flat balustrades are carved with the bodies of serpents and the four sides are formed of inset fascias carved with beautiful bas-reliefs depicting jaguars, eagles and Chacmool.

Temple of Venus

The Temple of Venus is a platform with 25 m sides, each with a central stair, at the top of which significant heads of serpents emerge.

The four walls of the temple contain bas-reliefs representing the symbol of Venus, the symbol of power, and a Quetzacoatl that emerges from the jaws of a splendid serpent, completely covered with plumage, with a forked tongue and the claws of a jaguar.

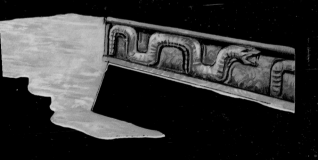

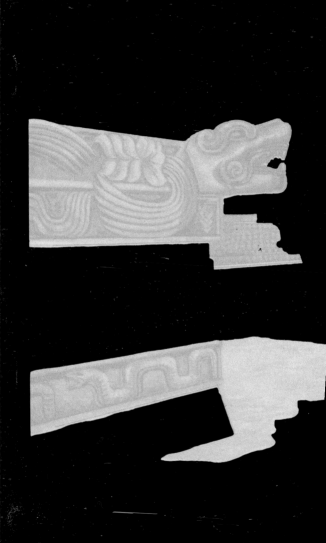

Plate 3 - Chichén Itzá: Tzompantli and the Temple of the Eagles

*At the top,
figure of Atlas,
showing the Toltec influence
in Chichén Itzá*

*On the right,
the Holy Well (Cenote)
with the ruins
of the steam bath*

Sacred Well

The Sacred Well or Cenote is 60 metres in diameter.

Its rocky walls descend 21 metres to reach the surface of the water, which in turn is another 20 metres deep.

The bottom is covered by 3-4 metres of mud and the water is coloured dark green by algae. On the south side of the Cenote there is a steam bath and some ruins that might be a flight of steps.

Pyramid of Kukulcan

The Pyramid of Kukulcan has a height of 24 metres and each side is of 55.5 metres. The body is formed of nine platforms, each smaller than the one before.

There is a stair of 91 steps on each of the four sides that represent the four cardinal points.

The dimensions of the pyramid represent the 365 days of the solar year.

The 91 steps of each stair also